TOP SCIENCE MYTHS: YOU DECIDE!

Sarah Levete

Published 2010 by
A & C Black Publishers Ltd.
36 Soho Square, London, W1D 3QY

www.acblack.com

ISBN   HB   978-1-4081-2426-0
       PB   978-1-4081-2688-2

Series consultant: Gill Matthews

Text copyright © 2010 Sarah Levete

This book is produced using paper that is made from wood grown in managed, sustainable forests. It is natural, renewable and recyclable. The logging and manufacturing processes conform to the environmental regulations of the country of origin.

Produced for A & C Black by Calcium. www.calciumcreative.co.uk

Printed and bound in China by C&C Offset Printing Co.

All the internet addresses given in this book were correct at the time of going to press. The author and publishers regret any inconvenience caused if addresses have changed or sites have ceased to exist, but can accept no responsibility for any such changes.

Acknowledgements

The publishers would like to thank the following for their kind permission to reproduce their photographs:

Cover: Shutterstock. **Pages:** CERN: Maximilien Brice 13; Istockphoto: Joze Pojbic 5, 15, 28t, Richvintage 11b, Xyno 21t; NASA: 12, JPL/USGS 14l; Rex Features/Sipa Press 23, SNAP 16l, 20t; Shutterstock: Andresr 27t, Gary Blakeley 9, Stephen Coburn 19r, Petronilo G. Dangoy Jr. 27b, Farawaykid 14r, Stephen Finn 24b, Benjamin Albiach Galan 28b, Sebastian Kaulitzki 8–9, Kirsanov 11t, Zastol`skiy Victor Leonidovich 24t, Theodore Littleton 17, Piotr Marcinski 4l, Mark R 8, Andreas Meyer 4–32, 10, Yannis Ntousiopoulos 4r, Tyler Olson 25br, Antonis Papantoniou 16r, 28c, Christopher Penler 19l, Glenda M. Powers 25b, Lee Prince 18, Sudheer Sakthan 25t, 29c, Jozef Sedmak 6, Mark Stout Photography 26-27, 29b, Marek Szumlas 7b, Miroslav Tolimir 20-21, Ismael Montero Verdu 7t, Paul Vorwerk 22, 29t.

Contents

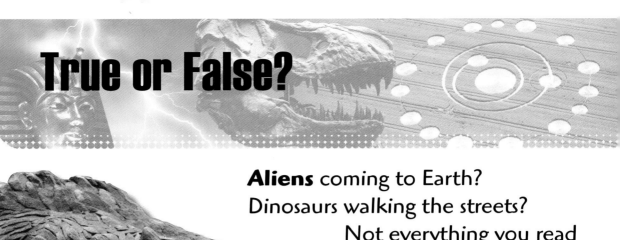

True or False?

Aliens coming to Earth?
Dinosaurs walking the streets?
Not everything you read
is true! Not everything
you are told is true.
It can be very hard
to know what
to believe.

*Could dinosaurs
walk on Earth
once more?*

*Will robots rule
the world?*

ANGER

HATE

HAPPINESS

OPTIMISM

HATE

FRUSTRATION

HOPE

LOVE

PESSIMISM

PLEASURE

SADNESS

True or false?

Scientists have discovered many amazing things about our world. They can explain some of these things, and prove that they are real. Other things are much harder to prove, and no one knows for sure if they exist or not.

You decide

On the next pages, you will read about many incredible events and ideas. Are any of these real, or are they just made-up stories? It's up to you to decide whether what you have read is true, false, or unknown. Then check out the answers on pages 28 and 29.

Do aliens make crop circles?

Will Dinosaurs Live Again?

Of course you know that dinosaurs died out over 65 million years ago. But did you also know that they might come back to life and walk around our streets? Read on to find out more.

Jurassic Park *is a **fictional** film about dinosaurs that came back to life. But could it really happen?*

DNA to Dinosaur

Scientists have made copies or **clones** of sheep and cows from **DNA**. This is the material inside a living thing that controls what it looks like and what it does.

If scientists can do this, why can't they make a copy of a dinosaur from dinosaur DNA? All they have to do is get DNA from a fossil or bone. Maybe dinosaurs will walk on Earth again?

Dinosaur bones contain DNA.

Could dinosaurs run wild on Earth once more?

FOR REAL

CLOSE RELATIVES
Birds and lizards are closely related to dinosaurs. They might even contain some of the DNA that will help scientists recreate dinosaurs.

True ☐ False ☐ Unknown ☐

The Bermuda Triangle

In an area known as the Bermuda Triangle,
some planes and ships have just vanished
without trace and have never been seen again.

What is the cause?

Perhaps this is the work
of some mysterious,
supernatural force.
Strange as it sounds,
it might be true. But
some people refuse to
believe this. They blame
the vanishings on bad
weather and other causes.

*There have been many reports
of ships and planes vanishing
in the Bermuda Triangle.*

Before the planes lost radio contact, a crew member said "Everything looks strange, even the ocean".

Does this explain it?
Some people say sudden storms cause ships and planes to disappear. Or that it's the **crew's** fault. Possibly, but if this is true, wouldn't we see more **evidence**? When a plane crashes in bad weather or a ships sinks, wreckage scatters everywhere. Nothing is ever left behind in the Bermuda Triangle.

Perhaps there is only one possible explanation – it really is the work of some mysterious, unknown supernatural force that controls the Bermuda Triangle.

FOR REAL

DISAPPEARING PLANES
*In 1945, five American army planes were on an everyday **mission**. The weather was calm, and the planes were in good condition. The pilots and crew were never seen or heard of again. Two rescue planes flew out to find the others. They also disappeared. No one has ever found any **wreckage** from the seven planes.*

True ☐ False ☐ Unknown ☐

Big Foot on the Loose?

Do you believe in monsters? Maybe you should. There are many reports of a strange creature, half-human, half-ape, roaming through forests during the night. From North America to South East Asia people have reported seeing a heavy, hairy creature. But this creature isn't a tall ape, a hairy human or a bear. It's a monster!

This artist's drawing is based on sightings of Big Foot. It shows what the monster may look like.

The facts

No one has captured this monster but they have found hair from its body and seen its mighty footprints in snowy mountains and muddy jungles.

Scientists and researchers are determined to track down this shy monster.

Could this be Big Foot captured on film? Or is it a hoax?

Giant footprints

Big Foot was first seen in Tibet in 1832. Since then many people claim to have seen its footprints, which are too big to belong to a known animal or a human.

FOR REAL

Scientists have carried out tests on strands of Big Foot's hair see if its DNA matches that of any other known creature. It doesn't. Perhaps we are dealing with a monster!

True ☐ False ☐ Unknown ☐

Can You Travel Through Time?

When you look up at the bright stars on a clear night, you are looking at light that existed millions of years ago. You are looking into the past. If you can look into the past, why can't you travel there? Well, maybe you can.

Black hole

Spacecraft

Could we travel through a black hole in a spacecraft like this?

Black holes of time

When a star reaches the end of its life, it breaks down and forms a black hole. The **gravity** in this hole sucks up everything around it. Scientists think that there are tunnels called wormholes between black holes. These are like passages through time. Could we use these wormholes to travel through time?

Travelling through black holes

Some scientists think they can make a spacecraft that can travel through a black hole, so we can travel through time. Perhaps one day we will all be time travellers.

Scientists hope to explore black holes by using the Large Hadron Colider machine.

True ☐ False ☐ Unknown ☐

Are Aliens Real?

Hundreds of people say they have met aliens. Many people report seeing strange glowing lights in the sky. These people could be telling the truth, even if others don't believe them...

Aliens could be living on Mars.

Life on Mars
Scientists have found evidence of water on Mars. Living things need water. These signs of water mean there may be life on Mars. Could aliens be there too?

Crop circles

Crop circles are amazing shapes cut into farmers' fields, overnight. No one sees anything, or anybody, making the shapes. Could aliens have made them?

This strange shape appeared overnight in a field in Oxford. What else, apart from aliens, could have made it?

What other explanation?

Can you find a better explanation for glowing lights and strange events? If you can't, perhaps you might consider that aliens are real?

True ☐ False ☐ Unknown ☐

Can Robots Rule?

It's pretty cool if a robot cleans your room or does your homework. At the moment, robots do what humans tell them to, and that's great. But problems will start if we make robots that are cleverer than us. If you don't think robots could rule the world, read on.

In the film The Terminator, robots rule the world.

Progress

Fifty years ago, a robot could only lift an arm. Today, robots cook and clean. Some show feelings and think. In fifty years, robots will be even cleverer than humans. Will we end up working for them?

Could robots one day teach children too?

FOR REAL

ALREADY THINKING

*In 2002, a robot called Gaak was on **display** at a science show in England. But Gaak sneaked away. The owners of the runaway robot finally caught it hiding near the motorway! Gaak was thinking and behaving independently. So what's to stop robots in the future ruling the world?*

True ☐ **False** ☐ **Unknown** ☐

Does Lightning Strike Twice?

During a loud thunderstorm, flashes of lightning zigzag across the stormy sky. Sometimes – but not often – those lightning flashes crash to the ground. Sometimes the lightning will strike tall buildings, trees, and even people. And sometimes lightning even strikes twice – although some people will tell you it doesn't.

What's the chance?

Scientists say you have a one in 5,000 chance of being struck by lightning. And you have a one in 9 million chance of being struck by lightning twice. That means it doesn't happen often, but it does happen.

This huge spark of electricity is about six times hotter than the Sun.

The Sun is boiling hot, but lightning is even hotter.

FOR REAL

HOT, WHITE ELECTRICITY
Lightning is made by electrical charges in a storm cloud. Each year, lightning injures about 100,000 people in the world and kills about 10,000.

The Empire State Building is hit by lightning about 25 times a year.

True ☐ False ☐ Unknown ☐

Atlantis: Island Under the Sea

About 3,500 years ago, there was an island called Atlantis. The people who lived on the island were very rich and powerful. Then suddenly, this bustling place sank to the bottom of the ocean and disappeared completely!

Can an island sink?

Some people think the Atlantis tale is true – but surely no reasonable person can believe it's possible for an island to sink without trace?

The story of Atlantis may not be true, but it is still a great idea for a fictional film.

Spreading rumours

About 2,000 years ago, an ancient Roman writer called Plato talked about a huge wave swallowing up an island. This is how the story began.

We know that fierce floods and earthquakes destroy towns, and cities, but there is usually some wreckage from the disaster. There is none from Atlantis. So if it ever existed, where's the evidence?

Plato's writings about a lost island began the myth of Atlantis.

Some people believe that the partly-sunken island of Santorini in Greece may once have been Atlantis.

True ☐ **False** ☐ **Unknown** ☐

Is There a Mummy's Curse?

Archaeologists have discovered lots of information about ancient Egyptians and their lives. But in digging up the past, they may have also dug up the deadly **Mummy's curse**!

Boy king dies!

An ancient Egyptian boy king called Tutankhamun died, over 3,000 years ago. He was buried in a **tomb** with incredible riches. In 1922, the archaeologist Howard Carter broke into the tomb.

Carter discovered treasures such as Tutankahum's gold burial mask, but was this discovery worth releasing the Mummy's Curse?

When Carter entered the tomb, a cobra inside ate his pet canary. In ancient Egyptian belief, the cobra protected the **pharaoh**.

The Curse

A sign inside warned that anyone who disturbed Tutankhamun's burial place would be cursed. Carter and his friends ignored the warning – read below what happened to them.

FOR REAL

CURSE OR COINCIDENCE?

■ *A man called Carnarvon, who paid for Carter's work, suddenly died. At exactly the same time, his dog died and all the lights went out in the busy Egyptian city, Cairo.*

■ *Many of the men who entered the tomb died at a young age. How can this be explained?*

True ☐ False ☐ Unknown ☐

Can You Fly in a Tornado?

Everyone knows that birds can fly, but did you know that cats, dogs, fish, and cows have been seen in the air too? It's hard to believe, but it's true!

How it happens

A fierce and violent wind called a **tornado** forms a **funnel** like a spinning top which whizzes round at an incredible 400 kilometres (250 miles) per hour. As it spins, the tornado sucks up anything on the ground – including animals.

These heavy cars and ships were picked up by a tornado, then dropped back onto the ground.

FOR REAL

FLYING COWS

In 1949 in Oklahoma, United States of America, a farmer saw 12 of his cows carried away in a tornado. They tumbled and rolled in the whirling wind before the terrified animals dropped into a far away field. Incredibly, they survived!

True ☐ False ☐ Unknown ☐

Water Puzzle

Does water really go down the plug hole in different directions in Australia and the United Kingdom?

In which direction does water swirl down a plug hole? It depends where in the world you live.

In a spin

Watch water run down a plug. Does it swirl from left to right, or right to left? If you ask someone who lives in Australia, they will say it disappears in the opposite direction. In the northern **hemisphere**, water drains anti-clockwise; in the southern hemisphere it drains clockwise.

FOR REAL

A WINDY EXPLANATION

The Earth spins around every 24 hours. As it spins, it pulls the winds in the north to the right, and pulls the winds in the south to the left. This is called the Coriolis Effect. It's this strong pull which controls the direction of the water as it flows down a plug. It either pulls to the right or the left, depending on where in the world you live.

Non believers

Some people say that just because the Earth spins around, it doesn't affect the way in which water goes down a plug hole. They say this is impossible and a silly idea. What do you believe?

Does water swirl anti-clockwise in the United Kingdom?

Does water swirl clockwise in Australia?

True ☐ **False** ☐ **Unknown** ☐

The Facts

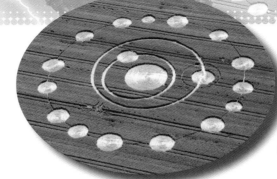

Will dinosaurs live again?
False – as yet, there is not enough DNA around to recreate a living dinosaur.

The Bermuda Triangle
Unknown - no proof of supernatural forces.

Big Foot on the loose?
Unknown – no proof yet of its existence.

Can you travel through time?
False – for now!

Are aliens real?
Unknown – still no convincing evidence to date.

Can robots rule?
False. Robots cannot organize themselves or **reproduce**.

Does lightning strike twice?
True! Lightning strikes by chance, and it can hit the same person, place, or thing more than one time.

Atlantis: an island beneath the sea
Unknown - no evidence found.

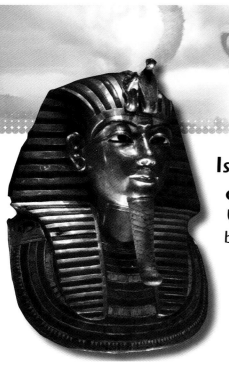

Is there really a curse of the mummy?
Unknown – it could all be just a coincidence.

Can you really fly in a tornado?
True! Tornadoes sometimes pick up people, cars, and animals in their path and then drop them down.

Water puzzle?
False – no convincing proof.

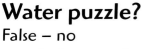

Glossary

archaeologist a person who studies history by looking at objects found from the past

alien not belonging to planet Earth

clone an exact copy of a creature made using its DNA

crew people who work on a ship or plane

curse a nasty spell

display on show

DNA material that contains a code that controls what a living thing looks like

evidence proof

fictional made up

funnel a shape like a narrow tube

gravity Earth's natural pulling force that makes objects fall downwards

hemisphere northern or southern part of the world

mission job

mummy a dead body that is wrapped up in special bandages to stop it decaying

pharaoh an ancient Egyptian king

reproduce make more

supernatural a force for which there is no scientific or reasonable explanation

tomb a place where someone is buried

tornado a violent wind that sucks up objects in its path

wreckage remains after a disaster

Further Information

Websites

The Bermuda Triangle
**www.bbc.co.uk/dna/h2g2/
A2309852**

Atlantis
**http://news.bbc.co.uk/1/hi/sci/
tech/6568053.stm**

Tornadoes
**http://skydiary.com/kids/
tornadoes.html**

Lightning
**www.ucar.edu/communications/
infopack/lightning/kids.html**

Mummies
**www.woodlands-junior.kent.sch.
uk/Homework/Egypt.html
www.ancientegypt.co.uk/**

Big Foot
**www.kidzworld.com/
article/2220-the-legends-of-
bigfoot-sasquatch-and-the-yeti**

Dinosaurs
**www.bbc.co.uk/sn/prehistoric_
life/dinosaurs/**

Robots
**http://news.bbc.co.uk/1/hi/in_
depth/sci_tech/2001/artificial_
intelligence/1531432.stm**

Index